Preface

The name of Richard the Lionheart is familiar to us all. Curiously, this legendary figure is more often associated with Aquitaine and the Holy Land than with Normandy.

The aim of this publication is to recount how Richard I, a worthy descendant of William the Conqueror, successfully maintained Normandy within the Plantagenet Empire, by constantly endeavouring to counter the ambitious plans of the King of France, Philip Augustus.

His violent and untimely death was to lead to Normandy's annexation to France. The Anglo-Norman territory, that "straddled the sea" and could well have offered an alternative to the national monarchic construction, was never to recover.

Contents

12th century lead casket, displayed in Rouen Cathedral and having contained the heart of Richard I.
Normandy Museum, Caen.

OREP
EDITIONS

15, rue de Largerie - 14480 Cully
Tel.: 02 31 08 31 08 - Fax: 02 31 08 31 09
E-mail: info@orep-pub.com - Website: www.orep-pub.com

Editor: Philippe PIQUE
Editorial assistant: Julie CLAVEL
Graphic design: OREP - Layout: Laurent SAND
English translation: Heather Costil

Front cover: *Richard the Lionheart, stained glass window in Portsmouth Cathedral. Courtesy of the Dean and the chapter of Portsmouth Cathedral.*

ISBN: 978-2-8151-0033-5 - Copyright OREP 2010
Legal Deposit: 2nd quarter 2010

A prestigious ancestry

During a period when princely families sought alliance through their heirs' matrimony, the future sovereigns were of an ancestry that combined the most prestigious of Christian Europe's families. Such was the case, more than any other, of Richard and his sibship, the descendants of Henry II Plantagenet, King of England, Duke of Normandy, and of the great Eleanor of Aquitaine: two legendary and central 12th century western figures.

Richard was born on the 8th of September 1157 in Oxford, where his father, Henry II, took up residence during his travels to England. However, Richard was not particularly fond of England and spent very little time there, essentially to collect the financial resources required to fund his interminable continental wars. Nevertheless, the English were much akin to this handsome and noble king, who left behind him a smell of sulphur and the memory of an unrivalled knight, engaging in the most perilous of battles.

Portrait of William the Conqueror, presented as a 16th century warrior king.
Anonymous, English, 19th century.
Private collection, all rights reserved.

Within what was still the Anglo-Norman world, Richard benefited from his ancestry which, by his grandmother Matilda "the Empress", dated back to William the Conqueror, hence ensuring him the Normans' respect and obedience.

Recumbent statue of Rollo, William the Conqueror's ancestor, in Rouen Cathedral. *Photograph Roger Jouet.*

From his mother, Eleanor of Aquitaine, and his grandfather Geoffroy Le Bel (the Handsome), Count of Anjou, he had inherited south-western roots, relishing in the troubadours' poetry and the fine carnal and sensual love, of which his other grandfather, William IX of Aquitaine, the "Troubadour", had been the forerunner.

As Henry II and Eleanor's fourth son, Richard was destined to become a court prince, a war leader as and when required, but by no means a sovereign.

However, the death of his two elder brothers, William at the age of three and, in particular, the flamboyant Henry the Young King in 1183, left him the heir apparent to the Plantagenet kingdom, much against the wishes of his father. His elder brother, Henry the Young King "prince of knighthood", had maintained such a

Recumbent statue of Richard the Lionheart's mother, Eleanor of Aquitaine, in Fontevraud Abbey.
Normandy Museum, Caen.

prestigious standing within the noble Anglo-Norman youth that Richard unremittingly endeavoured to outshine him by demonstrating is knightly prowess – at the head of his army in both the East and West – and his intellectual aptitude, by writing verses accompanied by the most illustrious troubadours.

The Plantagenet states and the Kingdom of France.

9th century engraving depicting Henry the Young King (1155-1183), Richard the Lionheart's elder brother and junior king, but with no genuine power, to his father Henry II.
Normandy Museum, Caen.

Matilda "the empress", "History of England" by the St Albans monks, 15th century.

3

A rebellious prince

Barely was he an adult that young Richard found himself at the heart of the incessant intrigue that reigned within his father Henry II's court. The Plantagenet empire was so vast that not a year went by without rebellion or frontier quarrels. Duke of Aquitaine as from 1174, Richard, who was not yet heir to the throne, only but rarely paid visits to Normandy: the title of duke was entrusted to his brother, Henry the Young King.

He was occasionally involved in signing peace treaties – none of them truly effective – between his father and the extremely pugnacious King of France, Philip Augustus. Thus, Richard learned the ropes of diplomacy and the psychological profile of he that was to become his worst enemy, Philip Augustus. These regular encounters between sovereigns were held on the outskirts of the regions of Île-de-France and Normandy, in the Vexin. This small region represented a genuine front line marking the border between the two kingdoms and upon which a great number of castles were built and relentlessly reinforced.

The fortified Château de Gisors was at the heart of such controversies since it was part of the dowry of Philip Augustus's sister, Aelis, whose hand had been promised to Richard since childhood. However, although the marriage

*Richard's homage to Philip Augustus for his continental fiefs, 18th November 1188: illumination taken from the **Grandes Chroniques de France**, 1450.*
Bibliothèque Équinoxe de Châteauroux. Reproduction CNRS-IRHT.

Ruins of the Château de Gisors.
Le livre du Millénaire de Normandie, *under the direction of Mr. Arnould Galopin and Mr. Schalck Faverie.*
Paris, 1911, p.48, cote FN C 25. Caen Municipal Library, Reproduction Ph. Dartiguenave.

was never to be, it was an unyielding source of conflict, each party exploiting poor Aelis and her dowry to his own political advantage.

Upon the death of Henry the Young King (1183), the title of Duke of Normandy legitimately fell upon Richard, as the eldest heir; however, due to these incessant quarrels with his father, he was to await the latter's death in 1189. Richard was finally crowned Duke of Normandy in Rouen on the 20th of July, then King of England on the 3rd of September 1189.

Château de Gisors. *Photograph S. W. Gondoin.*

Λ heart of lion or of leopard?

This epithet, which was to go down in history thanks to troubadour songs, appears to have always been Richard's. Barely was he 20 years old when Giraud de Barri – who surprisingly was not partial to him – referred to him as the Lionheart. Even William the Breton, chaplain to Philip Augustus, compared him to a lion.

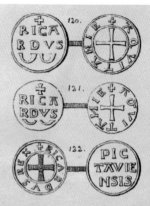

Richard I coins, engraved plate taken from Ducarel's Antiquités anglo-normandes, Mancel, 1823 Caen.
Calvados Departmental Archives.

The bravery and the valour that were readily attributed to the king of the animals, were perfectly in keeping with Richard's tumultuous life.

In the emerging field of heraldry during the second half of the 12th century, the lion was omnipresent, particularly among the Plantagenets. It would appear that Richard only truly adopted it in 1889, when he became King of England. On his return from the Crusades, he nevertheless had the two facing lions on his large royal seal replaced by three horizontal leopards, the reason for this change being unknown.

Richard the Lionheart's two shields, after his first seal (1189) and his second seal (1195). Birch, 1887 and Douet d'Arcs, 1868.

Although the Normans kept the leopards, England was to revert back to lions in the early 15th century. Hence, on both sides of the English Channel, the memory of Richard the Lionheart remained within the great diversity of the Plantagenet empire.

From left to right: The shield of John Lackland, Count of Mortain and Lord of Ireland (circa 1177-1180). Douet d'Arcq, 1863; Coat of arms of Richard I.

Richard the Lionheart depicted as a crusader.
Blondel Merry Joseph (1781-1853). Versailles, Château de Versailles, Château de Trianon. RMN.

Puppets depicting Charlemagne's knights from the **Opera dei Pupi.**
Palermo, Museo Internazionale delle Marionnette.

During the second half of the 12th century, Richard's years of learning coincided with the emergence of a new ideology: chivalry. It was to draw its roots from the very definition of the rights and the duties incumbent upon the prince – war leader – and consequently protector of the people. However, according to the Church, the prince was hence considered as a sinner, since he had drawn blood. Chivalry, through its code of honour soon to be reserved to the aristocracy, enabled this contradiction to be accepted as best possible, by legitimising war.

Sculpted capital from Montevergine (Campagna). Marble, 12th century. Capital originally from a cloister loggia. On one of its largest faces, it depicts two Norman knights duelling with spears. Normandy Museum, Caen.

The issue was far from a novelty, for even under William the Conqueror's reign, the Duke of Normandy's dynamic deeds, engaging in combat on the very front lines of his army, had aroused contradictory reactions. Although condemned by the Church, the fact that William led his men into battle, personally drawing blood, was on the contrary to arouse the chroniclers' admiration, for his greatness was far beyond that of Caesar himself: not only did he lead his army, but he was also an unparalleled warrior.

At Hastings, jugglers urged the Norman army into valiant combat, following William the Conqueror's example, alluding to the exploits quoted in the *Song of Roland.* Hence, this epic poem, a genuine ideological model, was to meet with undreamt of success throughout Europe, regional variations emerging from England to Spain and, of course, in the Court of Palermo. Mentioned for the very fist time in Hastings, written evidence in an Oxford manuscript dating from 1098 confirms the poem's Anglo-Norman origin.

On the battlefield, it led to the implementation of new combat techniques developed by the Normans and that were to ensure their military supremacy for many years. Magnificently illustrated by the Bayeux Tape-stry, the cleaving of foot soldiers and horsemen had become the rule on the battlefield.

Stamped ceramic paving representing a knight. Deux-Jumeaux, 14th century. Société des Antiquaires de Normandie collection, Normandy Museum, Caen.

Unparalleled knighthood

The technique involving a compact charge, spears lowered and directed horizontally, proved to be formidably effective; however, it required resources and much training, and was consequently a privilege reserved for the nobility.

To the above we can add the symbolic and almost religious status of weapons and, in particular, the sword (Excalibur is a fine example) in the knightly imagination.

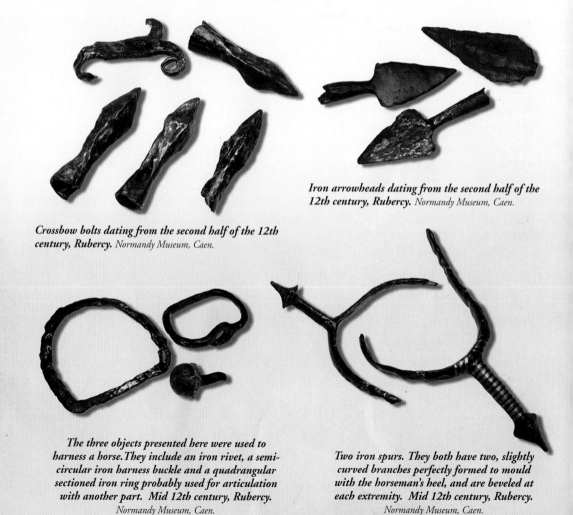

Iron arrowheads dating from the second half of the 12th century, Rubercy. Normandy Museum, Caen.

Crossbow bolts dating from the second half of the 12th century, Rubercy. Normandy Museum, Caen.

The three objects presented here were used to harness a horse. They include an iron rivet, a semi-circular iron harness buckle and a quadrangular sectioned iron ring probably used for articulation with another part. Mid 12th century, Rubercy. Normandy Museum, Caen.

Two iron spurs. They both have two, slightly curved branches perfectly formed to mould with the horseman's heel, and are beveled at each extremity. Mid 12th century, Rubercy. Normandy Museum, Caen.

Iron snaffle bit and fragment of a bridle bit, a simple beveled iron stem. Mid 12th century, Rubercy.
Normandy Museum, Caen.

Lost horseshoes are frequently unearthed on castral sites, bearing witness, along with harnessing parts, to the importance afforded to the equipment of horses. Mid 12th century, Rubercy.
Normandy Museum, Caen.

Horseshoe nails. Mid 12th century, Rubercy.
Normandy Museum, Caen.

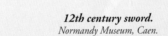

12th century sword.
Normandy Museum, Caen.

Norman horsemen charging. Reproduction of the Bayeux Tapestry, scene 19, 11th century.
Courtesy of the Town of Bayeux.

"He frolics so madly..." related Ambroise de Richard, who followed with delight the countless episodes of his master's amorous adventures. Much has been written on the subject, based either on flimsy witness reports or informed deduction that relied on reflection that is more appropriate to the present day than to the Middle Ages.

Thankfully, in his magnificent biography of Richard the Lionheart, the great medievalist Jean Flori successfully and objectively reunited available information without excessively exploiting its moral considerations. It is amusing to note the extent to which, even today, Henry II's clearly paedophile leanings, along with Richard's more than probable homosexuality, continue to plunge English historians into somewhat irrational opinions, in an endeavour to "protect" the memory of their distant sovereigns.

Richard died leaving no legitimate heir – although he is thought to have fathered an illegitimate son, Philip – and would appear to have expressed the greatest aversion to the idea of marriage. It is interesting to note that

Abbey of Fontevraud, chosen by Henry II Plantagenet as a royal abbey and the site of his dynasty's necropolis. Fotolia.

his betrothed, Aelis, Philip Augustus's half sister, resided within the Plantagenet court from a very young age and was very probably, whilst only a child, his father Henry II's mistress. In any event, Richard was to renounce their marriage, accepting to wed Berengaria of Navarre, for purely geopolitical reasons. He determinedly avoided poor Berengaria, with whom he is thought to, in fact, never have been intimate. Concurrently, his reputation as a womaniser compelled many a lord with whom he took up residence to hide any marriageable young girl and to offer him the most appealing servants

Recumbent statue of Henry II Plantagenet in the Abbey of Fontevraud. Normandy Museum, Caen.

Banquet scene. Reproduction of the Bayeux Tapestry, scene 3, 11th century.
Courtesy of the Town of Bayeux.

Berengaria of Navarre (1163-1230), Richard the Lionheart's wife.
Normandy Museum, Caen.

("He forcefully took the spouses, daughters and any other relatives of unmarried men...")

Available sources are far more explicit on his homosexual relationships which he was to publicly confess on at least two occasions, accompanying his declarations with repent-ance and punishment.

Firstly in Messina, before setting off for the Holy Land, Richard admitted the "repulsive ugliness" of his past existence, the chronicler Roger of Hoverden referring to "his sin". This reference cannot be to heterosexual relationships, a perfectly natural thing for a young and unmarried man who, in addition, was king!

Richard, when extremely poorly, offered even more explicit confessions upon his return from the Crusades in April 1195, referring to illicit copulation (*abjecto concubitu illicito*).

The subsequent reference to Sodom and Gomorrah leaves no doubt on the nature of his sin.

Thus, Richard would appear to have very probably been bisexual, with less of a paedophile penchant than his father, leading, be it in love or at war, an adventurous life.

The Tour des Archives (Archives Tower) in Vernon.
Photograph S.W. Gondoin.

As from the last decade of the IIth century, the overseas fever had struck the Occident. Beyond the Mediterranean, Jerusalem and Christ's tomb were the subject of incessant minor clashes between Christians and Muslims.

Guy of Lusignan, King of Jerusalem, was overthrown on the 4th of July 1187. Saladin's soldiers had captured the king and, what's more, the relics of the Holy Cross. Three months later, the Muslim troops entered Jerusalem, and in a rarely repeated gesture of mercy, the Saracens authorised the return of the Jews, maintaining the Christian cult in the Church of the Holy Sepulchre.

Richard the Lionheart and Philip Augustus quarrelling at Messina.
Chronique de France ou de Saint-Denis, 14th century. British Library.

Delivering the Holy Land was a duty for any Christian; however, the latent war between the Plantagenets and the Capetians was far from an incitement to leave. The crusade was costly, even if consequential exemptions were granted (remission of debt until the return...). As was his habit, Richard reacted fervently and without requesting his father's permission, he took to the cross in Tours. Fine battles and great prestige were in the making. Keen jugglers and troubadours were entrusted with the mission of galvanising the somewhat reluctant Norman and Angevin barons.

Philip Augustus, with ulterior motive in mind, was also preparing for action. The death of Henry II on the 6th of July 1189 delayed the departure, but was to give Richard increased confidence, for he was crowned King of England and Duke of Normandy.

Hence, when he joined Philip Augustus in Vézelay, two forceful sovereigns of comparable legitimacy headed for Jerusalem. Simultaneously, the Norman government was entrusted to the Seneschal Guillaume Fils-Raoul, a faithful and efficient follower of the Plantagenets.

The Anglo-Norman fleet headed for Gibraltar to join Richard in Salerno. The Duke of Normandy made slow headway in this other, unknown Norman territory, but within which he was familiar with the names of the occupying barons.

Before crossing the Strait of Messina, he stopped at Calabria, at the Mileto monastery, built by the first Norman conquerors. Once more, Richard came within a hair's breadth of death in a brawl that he had personally provoked.

The arrival of the Anglo-Normand fleet in the port of Messina proved to be a lavish affair. However, Messina was not Palermo; many Greeks had settled to the east of Sicily and their relationship with the Latins was deplorable: "For the town's middle-classes, a jumble of Greeks and ribald fellows, of Saracen origin, jeered at our pilgrims," Ambroise was to report.

Palermo Cathedral, built by the Normans in the 12th century. *Normandy Museum, Caen.*

Zisa Palace, Palermo. Built during the second half of the 12th century and a fine example of Arab-Norman art. Normandy Museum, Caen.

attempting to exploit the favours granted to the crusaders by the Sicilian kings to assert his power over the island.

Richard could well have taken advantage of the presence of his sister Joan, widow to William II, King of Sicily, to attempt to take the throne at Palermo, however other adventures awaited him in the East.

However, the renewal of ties between northern and southern Normans was not to be, for Tancred, the King of Sicily, submerged by a genuine dynastic tangle, speculated on whether the King of England was not

As the only Duke of Normandy to have set foot on Sicilian soil, Richard left behind him the memory of an arrogant and brutal Latin prince, showing but contempt towards the descendants of Robert Guiscard who had become "Christianised sultans" at the crossroads of Mediterranean populations.

Puppets depicting Norman knights and Saracen warriors. **Opera dei Pupi.**
Palermo, Museo Internazionale delle Marionnette.

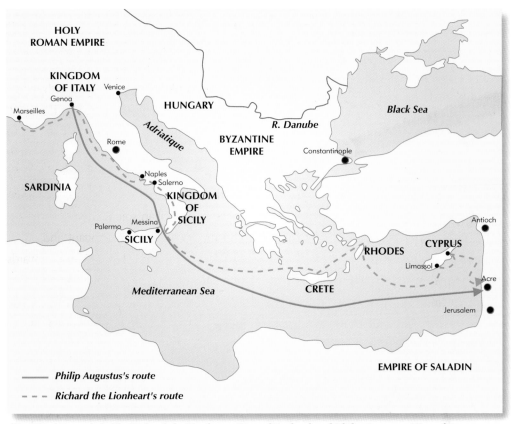

HOLY
ROMAN EMPIRE

KINGDOM
OF ITALY — Venice

Genoa

Marseilles

HUNGARY

Black Sea

Adriatique

Rome

R. Danube

BYZANTINE
EMPIRE

Constantinople

SARDINIA

Naples
Salerno

KINGDOM
OF
SICILY

Antioch

Palermo — Messina

SICILY

RHODES

CYPRUS

Limassol

Mediterranean Sea

CRETE

Acre

Jerusalem

EMPIRE OF SALADIN

——— *Philip Augustus's route*

- - - *Richard the Lionheart's route*

The Third Crusade led by Richard the Lionheart, King of England and Philip Augustus, King of France.

The century of tolerance that had been enjoyed throughout Sicily, this curious "Work of art State", very probably came to a close upon Richard's departure. The time had come for nation-states. Sicily and Normandy were no longer to enjoy independence.

Capital referred to as the "slaves capital", late 12th century. Bari Cathedral The central part is adorned with fiendish masks.
Normandy Museum, Caen.

Excalibur in Messina

Amidst the 12th century, at a time when the real and the fantastic were one, certain highly symbolic objects were to play the same role as that of the "*Chansons*". The transfer from myth to reality became almost tangible, via the posterity of a distinguished object, such as King Arthur's legendary sword: Excalibur.

Having no such illustrious ancestors as the Capetians' Clovis and Charlemagne, the Plantagenet kings sought stature in the very origins of English history, "inventing" King Arthur's tomb, miraculously unearthed during the reconstruction of the prestigious Glastonbury Abbey. At the foot of a giant skeleton (since great men were not to be confused with common mortals), a lead cross placed near to the body, bears the inscription, "Here lies the famous King Arthur, buried with Guinevere, his second wife, in the isle of Avalon," and the king's sword is placed alongside him.

Richard the Lionheart had brought the revered sword back from the Crusades. On the 4th of March 1191, he paid a visit to his cousin Tancred, the last Norman King of Sicily and, in Catania, he offered him "this admirable sword that the Bretons call Caliburn." In exchange for this exceptional

Saint Paul's head. Marble, mid 12th century, Messina. Example of the development of Sicilian Roman art. Normandy Museum, Caen.

and extraordinary gift, Tancred offered Richard 15 galleys to enable him to continue his journey. A royal offering comparable to the regular donation of precious relics between 12th century sovereigns.

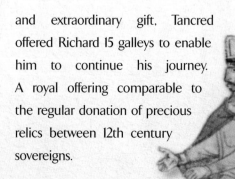

Tancred of Lecce, the last Norman King of Sicily. Liber ad honorem Augusti, Pietro da Eboli.

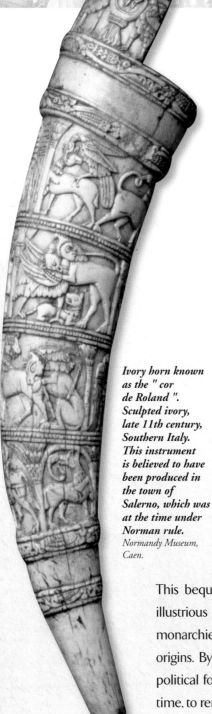

*Ivory horn known
as the " cor
de Roland ".
Sculpted ivory,
late 11th century,
Southern Italy.
This instrument
is believed to have
been produced in
the town of
Salerno, which was
at the time under
Norman rule.*
Normandy Museum,
Caen.

*Roland brandishing the Durandal sword,
abbey-church of Sainte-Marie-de-la-Règle,
Limoges, mid 12th century. Évêché Municipal
Museum, Limoges. The voussoir depicts a
knight with a hooded coat of mail and a
Norman-style helmet.*
Normandy Museum, Caen.

This bequest of one of the Anglo-Norman world's most
illustrious symbols was aimed at drawing the Norman
monarchies closer together by associating their mythical
origins. By doing so, Richard the Lionheart demonstrated
political foresight on a European scale that was, for a long
time, to remain unequalled.

The grand Christmas courts

The Nativity of Christ is a key event in the life of any Christian.

This time for peace and contemplation compels clemency and reflection. Hence, every Christmas, the Plantagenet kings, just like their German and French counterparts, reunited a grand court comprising not only their family, high dignitaries from the Church and their kingdom's leading lords, but also their matrimonial allies or often a rebellious vassal or two, looking to take advantage of the occasion to seek pardon or to regain their former rights.

It was also a time when, within the somewhat promiscuous context of these aristocratic gatherings, more or less lawful amorous bonds developed, and that were to influence political balance, much to the delight of the poetic jugglers.

Christmas courts were never organised two times running in the same place, for their aim was also for the king to be seen by his people throughout his entire and immense empire. Their cost was also so considerable for the welcoming castle and the town that

Caen castle today. *Normandy Museum, Caen.*

1. The Governor's Lodge (Normandy Museum).
2. The church of St Georges
3. The Hall of the Exchequer
4. The Old Palace
5. The Keep
6. Porte des Champs
7. Saint Peter's Gate
8. Fine Arts Museum
9. The Artillery Terrace
10. The Ramparts
11. Esplanade de la Paix

they could not be too frequently renewed. Nevertheless, each sovereign had his own preferences. Thus, Henry II, Richard the Lionheart and his successor, John Lackland, all carefully chose the place they were to spend Christmas and take a break from riding, often for over a month, a respite strictly reserved for the festive period.

Normandy, Maine and Anjou, the cradle of power, were the prime provinces for such courts. However, Henry II, who carefully nurtured his power over England, neglected neither London (Westminster) nor Oxford.

The most famous and very probably the most sumptuous of these courts was held at the Exchequer in Caen on the Christmas of 1182. Henry II, at the pinnacle of his power – but, as usual, at odds with his children – organised a genuine demonstration of power and family solidarity, in the company of his four sons, Henry the Young King, Richard, Geoffrey and

Porte des Champs, Château de Caen.
P. Leroux, Normandy Museum, Caen.

John. His daughters remained in England with their mother Eleanor of Aquitaine, kept in captivity by her husband and the most notable absentee at this family comedy. Only one of Henry II's daughters, Matilda, was present with her husband, the most eminent German

Hall of the Exchequer, Château de Caen. *Normandy Museum, Caen. Photograph P. Leroux and F. Decaens.*

prince, Henry the Lion, Duke of Saxony and of Bavaria, on their way to the Santiago de Compostela pilgrimage. Their court was so abundant that they took up residence in Argentan. Bertran de Born, a troubadour from Aquitaine who was bored to death in Caen, engaged (apparently successfully) in subjugating Matilda to whom he dedicated a famous poem.

Back in Caen, over a thousand knights jousted in the ducal castle and surrounding manor houses. To attain such a figure, the king had strictly forbidden any other Norman baron to hold a Christmas court.

From that date onwards, since confrontations with the King of France, Philip Augustus, were increasingly bitter, courts were often held in Normandy. The era of the courts of love, like the first held by Richard in 1176, had come to an end: courts had become increasingly political and less festive events. Thus, at the 1185 Christmas court in Domfront, Henry II learned of the demise of Baldwin IV, the Leper King of Jerusalem and of his proposed succession to the throne. For once on reasonably good terms with his son Richard, Henry refused the crown to devote himself to defending his existing continental possessions.

Château de Domfront. *Town of Domfront.*

Richard's first court as King of England and Duke of Normandy was held in 1189, in Bur in the Bessin area. The castle was relatively unknown, although it would appear to have played a considerable role during the late 12th century, and was probably unsuitable for such a vast gathering. Consequently, part of the court remained in Caen.

The poetic juggler Ambroise was present in Bur; of long-standing Anglo-Norman origin, he was preparing to accompany Richard on his crusade. He was disappointed to note that distraction was far from on the agenda, the *chansons de geste* and jugglers excluded, and that an atmosphere of contemplation prevailed. Richard appointed seneschals to govern over Normandy during his absence. However, he also needed to convince the barons to accompany him, for they were far less enthusiastic than they had been for the First Crusade. Bur was to welcome the Christmas court once more in 1196, in the midst of the war with France. Finally, Richard the Lionheart's last court was held in Domfront in 1198. It was a genuine council of war, for war was then total. Nearby in Vernon, Philip Augustus had reunited his own Christmas court to construct his plans to conquer Normandy.

Following Richard's death, the last breaths of the Anglo-Normand world led John Lackland to hold a major duke's court in 1202 in Caen, in an unsuccessful endeavour to obtain a peace conference with the King of France.

It is said that the king then fell into debauchery, perhaps in an attempt to forget his political ruin. Faced with such a heedless attitude, the inhabitants of Caen further grieved the demise of the late King Richard. The Capetians' hour had come.

Presentation from the 15th century temple and parish church of Saint-Siméon (Orne). Richard the Lionheart founded a priory at Saint-Siméon upon which the present-day parish church was later to be built. This sculpture was commissioned by canons from Richard the Lionheart's priory.
Normandy Museum, Caen.

The devil unchained

Such was the phrase used by the English chronicler Roger of Hoveden, and that Philip Augustus was, upon Richard's liberation, to announce to his brother John Lackland in the early days of February 1194. After fourteen months of captivity in Germany, where the Emperor had held him prisoner on his return from the Crusades, Richard was finally free. His liberation was made possible thanks to the payment of a huge ransom, gathered by his faithful followers, and the unyielding efforts of the queen mother Eleanor, despite her seventy years.

During Richard's absence, a legend was born, that of Robin Hood, that kind-hearted bandit who protected the poor from abuse from John Lackland, the de facto regent. Much later, Walter Scott's Ivanhoe was to undertake the defence of the poor whilst awaiting the return of the good king, torn from his people by a malevolent conspiracy.

Richard the Lionheart's seal. Deville, Histoire de Château-Gaillard et du siège qu'il soutint contre Philippe Auguste en 1203 et 1204, 1829, plate III.
Calvados Departmental Archives.

The siege of Château-Gaillard, winter 1203-1204,
Grande Chroniques de France *circa 1350.*
Municipal Library, Town of Castres.

Despite the fact the Richard spent very little time in England, he was, nevertheless, extremely popular there, continuing to offer the guarantee against expansionism and the Capetian enemy. Almost a century later, following William the Conqueror's expedition, the English people knew that they remained vulnerable to a new invasion. John Lackland's incompetence and cupidity with regard to his subjects did the rest.

Hence, Richard landed at Sandwich on the 13th of March 1194, to effortlessly regain the English throne. After having ensured that the nation's institutions were correctly run, and having reinforced power among his faithful followers, Richard left England on the 12th of May, never to return.

When he landed at Barfleur, he was welcomed with popular jubilation that was to continue at each step of his journey through Normandy as far as Rouen. The Normans were delighted to regain a duke capable of chasing out the King of France whose conquest of the dukedom had relentlessly progressed. Thus, for the very first time, the Capetians had conquered the Norman ports (Dieppe, Le Tréport), hence offering them an opening towards the English Channel.

Before resuming combat, Richard stayed in Lisieux to meet with his brother, John Lackland, who was literally terrorised at the idea of accounting for his multiple acts of treason towards his elder brother.

Undoubtedly under the influence of his mother Eleanor, Richard pronounced the famous quotation reported by the period's chroniclers, "Don't be afraid John, you are a child. You have fallen into bad company, and it is those who have led you astray who will be punished." Once the order of things restored, the time had come for the final conflict between the Plantagenet and the Capetian leaders. However, one thing had changed; what had formerly been but a traditional dynastic rivalry between two kings who had often ridden side by side and even feasted at the same table, was to become a deathly dual between two men driven by hatred. Richard could not forgive Philip's treason upon his return from their crusade, whereas Philip could no longer bear Richard's arrogance and military genius, which prevented the king from further expanding the Capetian kingdom.

To ensure recovery of the dukedom of Normandy, already partially occupied, Richard needed an impregnable stronghold between Rouen and Paris, and that stronghold was to be Château-Gaillard.

Richard on crusade.
French engraving,
19th century.
Calvados Departmental
Archives.

The ruins of Château-Gaillard. *Town of Les Andelys.*

" Is it from the ramparts of Messina, from Saint John's Church in Acre or from Dieterichstein that noble Richard was inspired for this admirable military architecture, of which no other example existed, and no imitation has been made here (…)? None of our medieval constructions had ever forebode such sublime character." This extract from *Voyages pittoresques et romantiques dans l'Ancienne France* (1820), the very first work devoted to cultural tourism and founded on historical memories, illustrates the importance that Château-Gaillard was to hold within the Norman's imagination, as a symbol of the Anglo-Norman resistance to the inexorable rise of the Capetian power.

The sheer speed of its construction, the colossal sums invested, the originality of its architecture, partly inspired by constructions seen in the Holy Land, all combined to make this castle a genuine exception.

Nonetheless, in the late 12th century, castles were far from lacking in the Vexin, this buffer zone that separated the Capetians from the Plantagenets. In the 1190s, French pressure was at its peak in eastern Normandy. Richard the Lionheart maintained a military and very probably financial advantage between his turbulent return from the Holy Land in 1194 and his death in 1199. It was during this period that, in order to reinforce the Norman frontiers and to turn heads, he undertook the construction of one of the Western world's most formidable fortresses.

Château-Gaillard is also one of the rare castles to be so well documented, and this is all the

Poster announcing the seventh centenary of Château-Gaillard, 1896. Léon Coutil, who designed the poster, chose to portray Philip Augustus's victory in 1204, rather than the castle's construction.
Cote 1 Fi 31.
Évreux, Eure Departmental Archives.

more surprising since it was built ex nihilo. We know, for example, based on accounts from the Normandy Exchequer dating from 1198, that Richard spent, the same year, some 9,417 livres and 18 sous for Château-Gaillard, a cost well over the maintenance of all of his other castles combined. In their chronicles, Philip Augustus's two biographers, Rigord and William the Breton, devoted much attention to the siege of Château-Gaillard. This choice was both a political and a military one – for the castle – bequeathed by Richard the Lionheart and forsaken by his brother and successor John Lackland – was very quickly to become a symbol. The fall of Château-Gaillard was to mark Philip Augustus's triumph and led to the almost effortless surrender of the remaining Norman towns. The fortress that dominated the right bank of the Seine at the 100 metre summit of a rocky crag, was the very heart of a military and residential complex including a series of fortified strong points.

The Andelys peninsula housed, over and above the castle itself, two advanced enclosures located upstream and downstream, a fortified residence on an island on the River Seine equipped with two bridges and a vast enclosure round the village of Petit Andely.

The fortress was an elaborate construction due to the rocky relief of the outcrop upon which it stood. It was isolated from the plateau by a huge, 20 metres high ditch, hollowed out of the chalky foundation.

Two enclosures, flanked with several circular towers and fine stonework buttresses, offered solidity to the overall construction. The circular keep, which measured 19 metres in diameter at its base, and 14.5 metres at its summit, was over 20 metres high.

The festooning on the keep enclosure and curious machicolations on arches, realistically reproduced by Viollet-le-Duc, were of Palestinian inspiration.

Despite all of the above, the siege during the winter of 1203-1204 was to overcome the castle's defences. Little by little, the enclosure towers collapsed under the incessant attacks by the sappers, until the citadel and its keep were totally within the hands of Philip Augustus on the 6th of March 1204, the date that marked the surrender of the last defenders, who had lost all hope of assistance.

Over the following weeks, for better or for worse, Normandy gradually became French.

Les bouches inutiles, 1884, *Francis Tattegrain, oil painting. Scene of the siege of Château-Gaillard by Philip Augustus. The painting depicts the sustained agony of the non-combatants, "bouches inutiles" (useless mouths), expelled from the fortress.*
Town of Nantes, entrusted to the Town of Les Andelys.

Richard I the Lionheart, also known as Richard the Fearless.
Statue in Place Guillaume le Conquérant in Falaise. OREP.

It was with this imprecation that the Normans had welcomed Richard upon his liberation, such was their great fear of the French. Everyone was perfectly aware that Philip Augustus had taken advantage of Richard's absence to perfect his military strategy in Normandy, hence gaining ground.

Fighting had resumed elsewhere; in Touraine, Périgord and Aquitaine, the diversion of conquering towns and castles, of forming allegiance with then betraying the local barons, was pursued according to the rules of chivalry that had gradually been established over the previous two centuries.

In Normandy, the stakes had become consid-erable: over and above the dukedom's symbolic value within the Anglo-Norman state, the Seine valley was of vital economic and strategic importance, as clearly demonstrated by the English historian, John Gillingham. The King of France needed to take control of this territory to guarantee economic and commercial development for nearby Paris.

Over the last years of the 12th century, fighting took place simultaneously on all fronts. Such intense hostility was to be seen nowhere other than in Normandy. Every castle, every village, every strategic height was the theatre of bitter combat. Although relatively uncommon at the time, since less costly in terms of human lives and far more chivalrous, the control of the Seine's bridges, where attrition warfare and buying back prisoners were preferred, was nevertheless to lead to deadly campaigns.

Richard's military situation remained complicated due to the great lack of spirit with which John Lackland had defended Normandy. In February 1194, the Normandy Vexin was under French power and a garrison

Falaise Castle's three keeps, seen from the south-west.
Photograph François Trouillet, Town of Falaise.

occupied Évreux and, in particular, the fortress of Vaudreuil, barely a dozen kilometres from Rouen, was in the hands of the King of Paris. This castle, which was cherished by the Norman dukes since it was endowed with the privilege of housing the royal treasure, as were Caen, Falaise and Rouen, was to be at the very heart of the two kings' military strategy.

However, it was evident that the French and Plantagenet forces were well balanced, each adversary having relatively equivalent military and financial resources at their disposal. A truce proved to be de rigueur, hence leaving each of them the time to consolidate his power and to reinforce his army by recruiting new troops. However, the truce was only to sustain the situation for a few months before the inevitable resumption of combat. Such was the case of the famous truce signed on the 23rd of July in Tillières by representatives of both kings. For Richard, this situation was unbearable: it led to the progression of the French troops on Normandy's entire eastern frontier, hence confirming Philip Augustus's control of several castles including Gisors and Verneuil.

But the so-called truce was to continue up to the 1st of November 1195. Nevertheless, it was cunningly utilised to dismember the castles yet to be surrendered, or to fortify sites which had hitherto remained outside the battle zone. Thus, Philip Augustus had the ramparts of

Philip II, known as Philip Augustus, King of France (1165-1223). Painting by Louis-Félix Amiel, currently displayed in Versailles.
Château de Versailles and Château de Trianon.

Vaudreuil razed to the ground and destroyed the Portejoie bridge over the Seine, whilst beating the retreat.

Normandy, a hitherto rich dukedom, was bled white by this devastating military pressure; from destroying harvests to pillaging, both armies had severely impoverished the land.

Philip Augustus also took advantage of the truce to reinforce his military positions on other fronts and to besiege the fortification of Issoudun, a strategic site for the control of the province of Berry. Richard immediately travelled to Berry himself with his English

How Philip Augustus chased out King Richard.
Illumination taken from **the Grandes Chroniques de**
France, circa 1375-1379. *Bibliothèque nationale de France.*

The key features of his military strategy can been found in this treaty: rendering the network of castles increasingly dense and developing coalitions, even if at the cost of considerable generosity, as he did with Baldwin of Flanders, whose support he desperately needed on the northern border. The treaty, which was theoretically concluded for 18 months, was in reality to resist no longer than its predecessors.

Philip Augustus – just like Richard – personally took part in combat, even when it involved but minor skirmishes. And it was precisely during one of such encounters that, when attempting to escape from Richard's men who were on the verge of taking him prisoner, the King of France had a close brush with death when the wooden bridge of the Château de Gisors gave way under the weight of the French knights in their haste to take refuge inside. He was saved just in time from drowning, to immediately regain control of defensive operations.

knights, those seasoned warriors that accompanied him on all fronts, whereas the Normans dared not abandon their persistently threatened province.

On the 5th of December 1195, the two kings resigned themselves to accepting the principal of a peace conference. It was to be held after the Christmas courts between Vaudreuil and Gaillon, in the very heart of the conflict. The peace treaty, which was meticulously precise, demonstrated that, since his return, Richard had recaptured a great number of castles and had reclaimed his authority over several minor lords within the frontier zone, who were quite used to bargaining their support with one or other of the belligerents.

Such personal commitment on the part of the sovereign in simple, yet life-threatening "surprise attacks", at times when major European political balance was at stake, may appear to us as somewhat foolhardy, but such was the feudal world. A few months later, when fighting was at its pinnacle, Richard was to be far less fortunate than Philip Augustus...

It was in Chalus-Chabrol near the town of Limoges that the last episode in the tumultuous life of the Lionheart was to be played. Achard, the lord of the manor and Count of Chalus, was in possession of a treasure that had been unearthed by a peasant, comprising a "golden table", a silver shield and several ancient medals. The treasure aroused Richard's curiosity, for he had always nurtured a predilection for precious metals. He was looking to apply the Normandy custom in favour of the sovereign, in order to recover all of the riches found.

Failing to reach a rapid agreement, he set up siege before this small and poorly defended castle as he had done so often. It was during his inspection of the castle's defences that he was hit in the shoulder by a crossbow bolt. He audaciously cried out a compliment to the crossbowman and returned to his tent. However, this time his wound did not heal and Richard very quickly realised that death was imminent. He sent for his mother, Queen Eleanor, who was to accompany him up to his last breath. Thus, he who had led some of the most glorious battles in the entire history of western chivalry, was to lose his life in a mediocre skirmish, following an injury that was initially judged by his personal surgeon as benign.

According to his last will, the royal remains were transported to the Abbey of Fontevraud. As King, his last duty was towards his subjects. Hence, his heart was transported to Rouen and his entrails buried in Fontauvraud.

As the focal point of the Anglo-Norman power, Rouen had always been faithful to Richard and it was in recognition of such loyalty that the King's heart was buried in the cathedral "in the sanctuary next to the epistle". The grave representing Richard lying in his royal costume was destroyed in 1734. Only the lead casket containing fragments of fabric were recovered. An engraved inscription in 12th century lettering reveals its contents: *Hic jacet, cor Ricar, di regis, Anglorum.*

Recumbent statue of Richard the Lionheart in Rouen.
OREP.

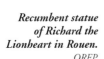

The day-to-day life of a Norman lord

Under Richard's reign

In the late 12th century, written sources were increasingly abundant, but they offered little information on the life of medieval men. Throughout research, only archaeology has occasionally been able to open windows on the day-to-day lives of our forefathers.

Hence, it was by a great stroke of luck that, in the 1970s, the archaeologist Claude Lorren was allowed to excavate the dwelling place of an Anglo-Norman family from the mid-aristocracy. He fortuitously discovered, within the commune of Rubercy to the west of Bayeux, at the confluence of two rivers, the seigneurial residence of Hugues Wac. The Lord of Rubercy (deceased circa 1175) had participated in the long civil war that had ravaged England in the middle of the century. In return for his loyal service, he was offered the hand of a rich heiress from the County of Bourne (near Lincoln) and their possessions were scattered on both shores of the English Channel.

His residence was made of wood and was surrounded by an enclosure before which a ditch had been hollowed. The residence was rebuilt in stone by his son. This small château endowed with minimal defences, ancestor to the typical Norman manor houses that were to follow, offered a wealth of everyday objects, costumes, riding equipment and games pieces, all of them bearing witness to the day-to-day life of a lord at the turn of the 13th century.

Of no lesser archaeological importance, the capitals and sculpted stones also offer precious proof of decorative customs on civil buildings.

Huges Wac's grandson, Baldwin, who was a faithful follower of Richard, then of his brother, John Lackland, had his belongings confiscated by Philip Augustus in 1204 and he fled to England. His abandoned place of residence was to become, eight centuries later, an undreamt of archaeological deposit.

Ruthery (Calvados), scale model of the 12th century seigneurial residence. Normandy Museum, Caen.

Wrought iron casket keys, second half of the 12th century, Rubercy (Calvados). Normandy Museum, Caen.